VOLUME 6: 1980–1990

Songs That Define an Era

Alfred

ISBN-10: 0-7390-4216-5
ISBN-13: 978-0-7390-4216-8

Contents

AFTER ALL
(Love Theme from "Chances Are")

Words and Music by
DEAN PITCHFORD and
TOM SNOW

After All - 5 - 1

4

straight.

She: E/G#   A(9)

I still re-mem - ber___ when

C#m7   F#m   E/G#

your kiss was so___ brand new.   Ev- ery mem-o-ry___ re-peats,___ ev- ery

A   E/G# Both: A   B   A/B B

step I take___ re-treats.___ Ev- ery jour-ney al - ways brings me back___ to you.___ Af- ter

cresc.

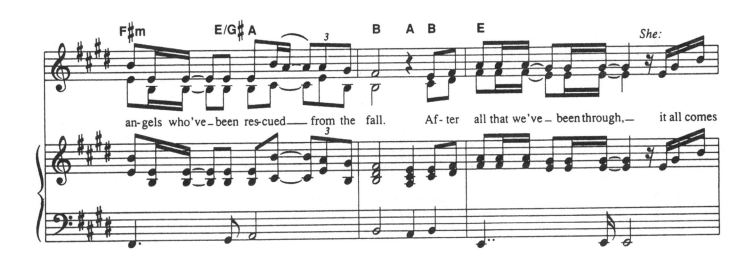

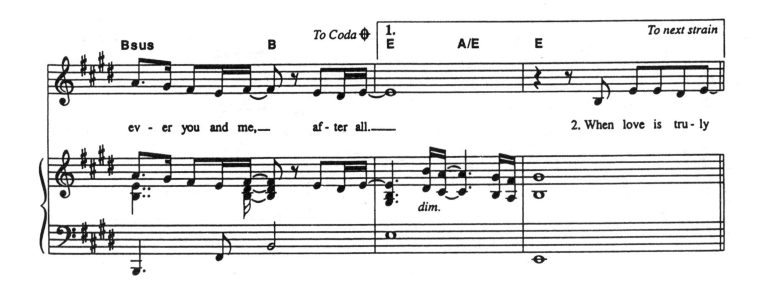

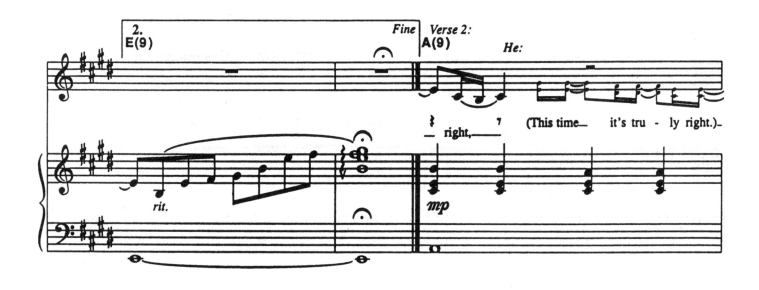

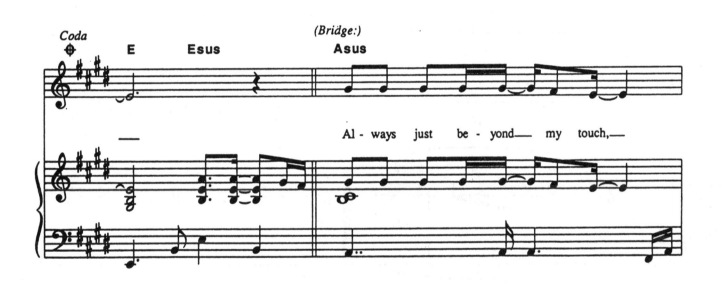

ARTHUR'S THEME
(Best That You Can Do)

Words and Music by
BURT BACHARACH, CAROLE BAYER SAGER,
CHRISTOPHER CROSS and PETER ALLEN

Once in your life, you'll find
Ar - thur, he does what he

Arthur's Theme - 4 - 1

10

self,   hey,   what - 've I found?
way   they   want him   to be.

When you get caught be-tween the moon   and   New York   Cit - y,

I know it's cra - zy,   but it's true.___

If you get caught   be - tween the

Arthur's Theme - 4 - 3

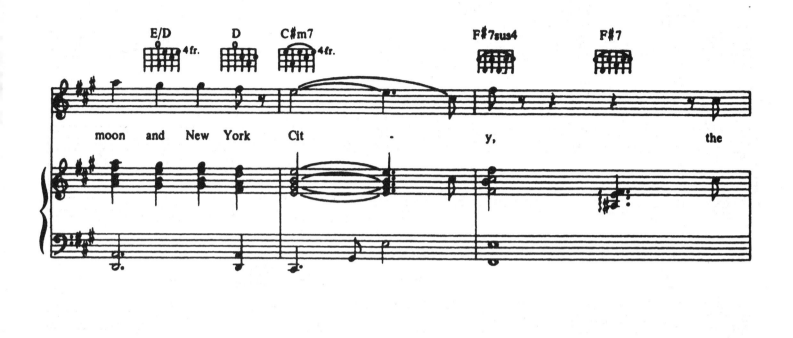

ALWAYS

Written by
JONATHAN LEWIS, WAYNE LEWIS
and DAVID LEWIS

Always - 3 - 1

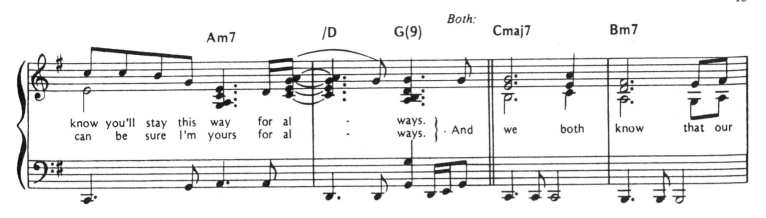

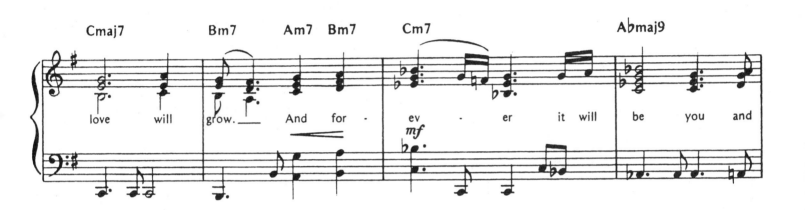

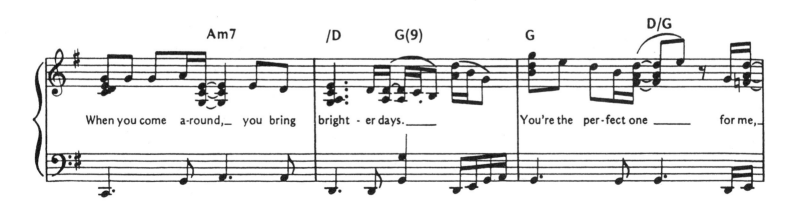

1. D.S. %

_____ and you for-ev-er will be. And I will love you so for al - ways.

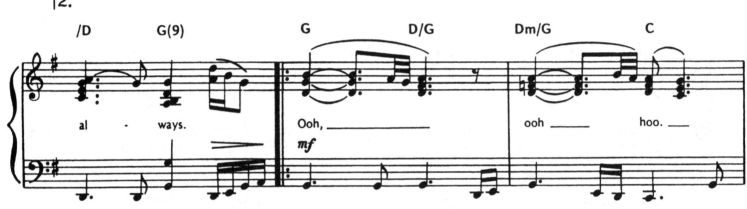

2.

al - ways. Ooh, _____ ooh _____ hoo. _____

_mf_

Repeat ad lib. and fade

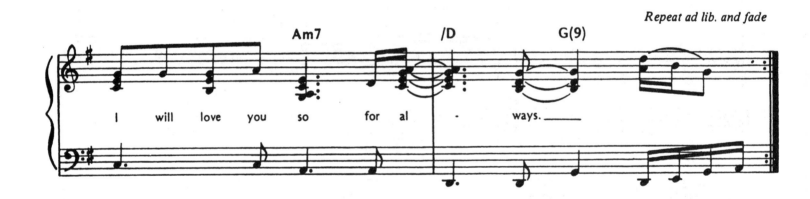

I will love you so for al - ways. _____

BACK IN THE HIGH LIFE AGAIN

Words and Music by
STEVE WINWOOD and
WILL JENNINGS

Moderately, with a beat

It used to seem to me that my life ran on too fast, and I
used to be the best to make life be life to me, and I

had to take it slow - ly just to make the good parts last. But
hope that you're still out there and you're like you used to be. We'll

Back in the High Life Again - 5 - 1

16

when you're born to run____ it's so hard to just____ slow down, so
have our-selves___ a time,____ and we'll dance till the morn-ing sun, and we'll

don't be sur-prised to see____ me back in____ that bright part of town.__ I'll
let the good times come___ in and we won't stop un-til we're done.__ We'll} be

back in___ the high - life a - gain.___ All the doors___ I closed___

___ one time___ will o-pen up a-gain. {I'll We'll} be back in___ the high life a-gain.___

BEAT IT

Written and Composed by
MICHAEL JACKSON

They told him, "Don't you ev - er
They're out to get you. Bet - ter

come a - round here. Don't wan - na see your face; you bet - ter dis - ap-pear."
leave while you can. Don't wan - na be a boy; you wan - na be a man.

The
You

Beat It - 3 - 1

BORN IN THE U.S.A.

Words and Music by
BRUCE SPRINGSTEEN

Repeat ad lib. and fade

Verse 2:
Got in a little hometown jam,
So they put a rifle in my hand.
Sent me off to a foreign land
To go and kill the yellow man.
(To Chorus:)

Verse 3:
Come back home to the refinery;
Hiring man says, "Son, if it was up to me."
Went down to see my V.A. man; he said,
"Son, don't you understand, now?"
(To Instrumental Chorus:)

Verse 4:
I had a brother at Khesan,
Fighting off the Viet Cong;
They're still there, he's all gone.
(To Chorus:)

Verse 5:
He had a woman that he loved in Saigon,
I got a picture of him in her arms, now.

Verse 6:
Down in the shadow of the penitentiary,
Out by the gas fires of the refinery;
I'm ten years burning down the road,
Nowhere to run, ain't nowhere to go.
(To Chorus:)

BROKEN WINGS

Words and Music by
RICHARD PAGE, STEVE GEORGE
and JOHN LANG

Medium Fast Rock

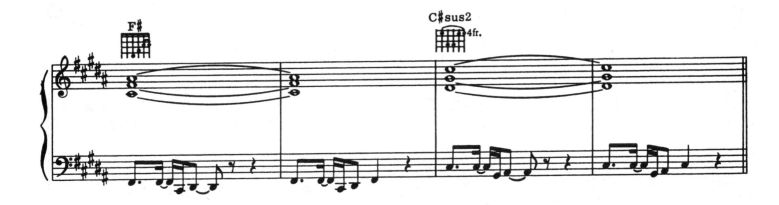

Ba - by,___ don't un - der - stand why we
Ba - by,___ I think to - night we can

Broken Wings - 5 - 1

can't just__ hold__ on   to each oth-er's   hands._____
take what__ was__ wrong   and make__ it   right._____

This time__   might be the last   I   fear,   un-less I__   make it
Ba - by,__   it's all I   know,   that you're half of the   flesh   and

28

30

CARELESS WHISPER

Words and Music by
GEORGE MICHAEL and ANDREW RIDGELEY

Lyrics:

I feel so un-sure_
Time can nev-er mend_
To-night the mu-sic seems so loud,_ I

_ wish that we_ could lose this crowd,
_ as I take your hand_ and lead you
the care-less whis-per
may-be it's bet-ter this way, if we'd

CELEBRATION

Words and Music by
RONALD BELL, CLAYDES SMITH, GEORGE BROWN,
JAMES TAYLOR, ROBERT MICKENS, EARL TOON,
DENNIS THOMAS, ROBERT BELL and EUMIR DEODATO

Celebration - 3 - 1

CRAZY FOR YOU

Words and Music by
JOHN BETTIS and JON LIND

Crazy for You - 5 - 1

DON'T YOU WANT ME

Words and Music by
PHIL OAKEY, ADRIAN WRIGHT and JO CALLIS

Additional Lyrics

3. I was working as a waitress in a cocktail bar,
   That much is true.
   But even then I knew I'd find a much better place
   Either with or without you.

4. The five years we have had have been such good times,
   I still love you.
   But now I think it's time I live my life on my own.
   I guess it's just what I must do.

ENDLESS SUMMER NIGHTS

Words and Music by
RICHARD MARX

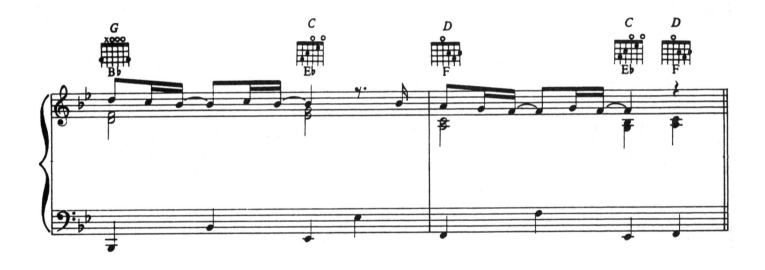

Sum-mer came_ and went_ with-out_ a warn - ing.
still re - call_ the walks_ a - long_ the beach - es, and the

Endless Summer Nights - 5 - 1

how the cit - y does - n't look_ the same._ _____ I'd
Ev - 'ry sin - gle breath_ you took_ was mine._ _____

give my life_ for one_ more night_ of hav-ing you here_ to hold_ me tight._ Oh_ please,_
We can have it all_ a - gain._ Say that you'll_ be with_ me when_ the_ sun_

take me there_ a - gain._ Oh,_____ oh._____
brings your heart_ to_ mine._ Oh,_____ oh._____

And I_____ re - mem - ber how_ you loved_

50

Endless Summer Nights - 5 - 5

FLASHDANCE... WHAT A FEELING

Words by
KEITH FORSEY and IRENE CARA

Music by
GIORGIO MORODER

52

54

now_____

(life)_____

What a feel - ing._____

FAITH

Words and Music by
GEORGE MICHAEL

Brightly, with a beat

Well, I guess it would be

nice
-by,
instrumental

if I___ could touch your bod - y.
I know___ you're ask - ing me___ to stay.

I know not
Say please, please,

ev - 'ry - bod - y
please don't go___ a - way.

has got a bod - y like
You say I'm giv - ing you the

you.___
blues.___

Oh,

May - be

but I got - ta think
be

Faith - 4 - 1

twice

be - fore___ I give my heart___ a - way. And I know
you mean ev - 'ry word___ you say. Can't help but

F   C

all the games___ you play be - cause I play them too.___ Oh, but I
think of yes - ter - day and an - oth - er who tied me down to___ lov - er - boy rules. *(2,3.)* Be -
Instrumental ends

F   C

need some___ time___ off from that e - mo - tion,___
fore this___ riv - er be - comes an___ o - cean,___ be -

F   C

time to pick___ my heart___ up off___ the floor.___ Oh, when that
fore you throw___ my heart___ back on___ the floor,___ Oh,___ oh, Ba - by, I'll

THE HARLEM SHUFFLE

Words and Music by
BOB RELF and EARL NELSON

The Harlem Shuffle - 3 - 1

Verse 2:
You scratch just like a monkey, yeah, you do - real cool.
You slide it to the limbo - yeah. How low can you go?

Now come on, baby, don't fall down on me now.
Just groove it right here to the Harlem Shuffle. *(To Chorus:)*

Verse 3: (key of A minor)
Yes, we hitchhike, baby, across the floor.
Whoa, whoa, whoa, I can't stand it no more.

Now come on, baby, now get into your slide.
Just ride, ride, ride, little pony, ride.

Chorus:
Yeah, yeah, yeah, do the Harlem Shuffle.
Yeah, yeah, yeah, do the Harlem Shuffle. (Do the monkey shine.)
Yeah, yeah, yeah, shake a tail feather, baby.
Yeah, yeah, yeah, shake a tail feather, baby.
Yeah, yeah, yeah, do the Harlem Shuffle. *(Repeat and fade)*

HIGHER LOVE

Words and Music by
STEVE WINWOOD and WILL JENNINGS

Higher Love - 5 - 1

love come o - ver me. Let me feel how strong it could be.___

No chord

Oh.___

Repeat and fade (vocal ad lib)

Bring me a high - er__ love, bring__ me a high - er__ love, whoa.__

Bring me a high - er__ love, bring me a high - er__ love..

Higher Love - 5 - 5

HOLD ON TO THE NIGHTS

Words and Music by
RICHARD MARX

Just when I ___ be - lieved ___
How do we ___ ex - plain ___

I could - n't ev - er want ___ for more, ___
some-thing that took us by ___ sur - prise? ___

70

*Vocalists: Hold C for 4 beats.

Hold on to the Nights - 6 - 3

72

some - one I've_ been search - ing for_ is right there._____

Hold on _ to the nights._

Hold on _____ to the mem - o - ries._____

I wish that I could give you more._____

Oh._____

Hold on ____ to the nights.____

HOW WILL I KNOW

Words and Music by
GEORGE MERRILL, SHANNON RUBICAM,
and NARADA MICHAEL WALDEN

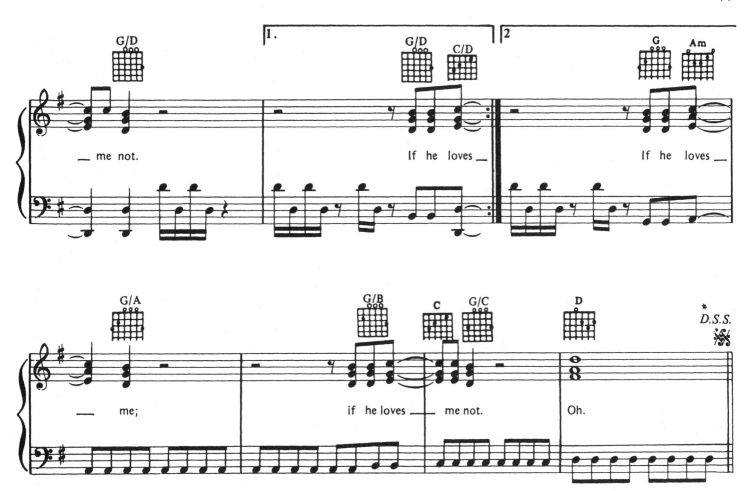

Verse 3:
Oh, wake me, I'm shakin'; wish I had you near me now.
Said there's no mistakin'; what I feel is really love.
How will I know? (Girl, trust your feelings.)
How will I know?
How will I know? (Love can be deceiving.)
How will I know?

Repeat Chorus in key of "E"

I KNEW YOU WERE WAITING
(FOR ME)

Words and Music by
DENINIS MORGAN and
SIMON CLIMIE

I Knew You Were Waiting - 4 - 1

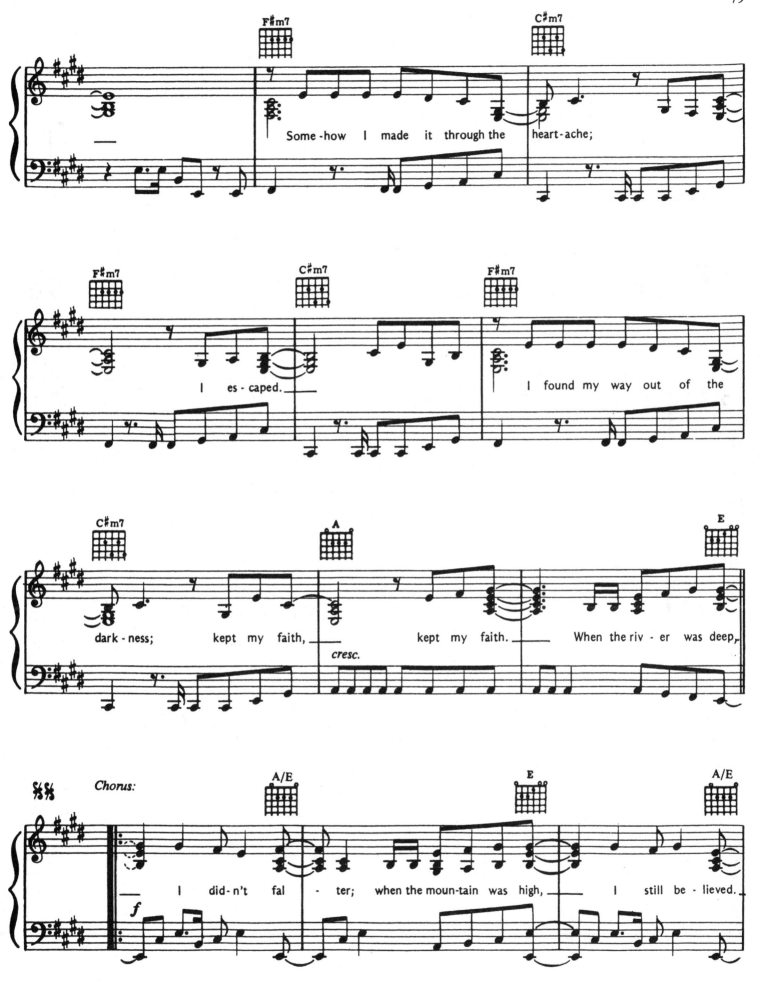

Bridge:

to-geth-er through des-ti-ny.

I know this love_ we_ share_ was meant to be._

I knew you were wait-ing,

knew you were wait-ing,

knew you were wait-ing for me._

D.S.S.

Verse 2:
With an endless desire, I kept on searchin', sure in time our eyes would meet.
Now like bridges on fire the hurt is over, one touch and you set me free.
I don't regret a single moment, oh, oh, lookin' back,
When I think of all those disappointments, I just laugh.
(To Chorus:)

IF YOU ASKED ME TO

Words and Music by
DIANE WARREN

Chorus:
Cmaj7
Em7/A
Gmaj7/A
G(9)
D(9)
I said I'd nev-er let no-bod-y in. But if you asked me to, I just might
G(9)
D(9)
G
G(9)
D(9)
change my mind and let you in my life for-ev - er. If you asked me to, I just might
G(9)
C(9)
To Coda
give my heart and stay here in your arms for - ev - er. If you
D(9)
C(9)
Gm/C
D(9)
C(9)
D5
asked me to, If you asked me to.

Verse 2:

MANEATER

Words by SARA ALLEN,
DARYL HALL and JOHN OATES

Music by
DARYL HALL and JOHN OATES

Maneater - 3 - 1

88

Maneater - 3 - 3

MORNING TRAIN
(Nine to Five)

Words and Music by
FLORRIE PALMER

Morning Train - 3 - 1

THE ONE YOU LOVE

Words and Music by
GLENN FREY and JACK TEMPCHIN

The One You Love - 4 - 1

cry when they know they've lost __ you. Some-one's gon-na thank the stars a - bove. __

What you gon - na

D.S. 𝄋 and fade

OWNER OF A LONELY HEART

Words and Music by
TREVOR RABIN, JON ANDERSON,
CHRIS SQUIRE and TREVOR HORN

THAT'S WHAT FRIENDS ARE FOR

Words and Music by
CAROLE BAYER SAGER and BURT BACHARACH

That's What Friends Are For - 3 - 1

SOMEBODY'S BABY

Words and Music by
JACKSON BROWNE and DANNY KORTCHMAR

TAKE MY BREATH AWAY

By GIORGIO MORODER
and TOM WHITLOCK

Take My Breath Away - 4 - 1

Take My Breath Away - 4 - 4

WE ARE THE WORLD

Words and Music by
MICHAEL JACKSON and LIONEL RICHIE

Moderately slow

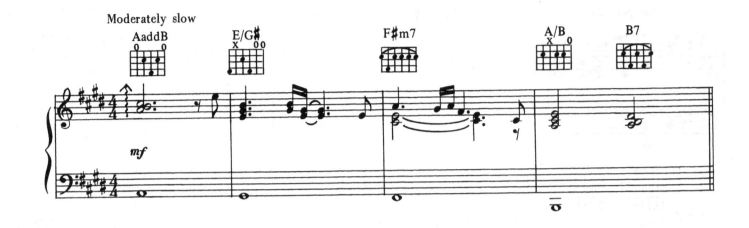

There comes a time _____ when we heed a cer - tain call, _____ when the

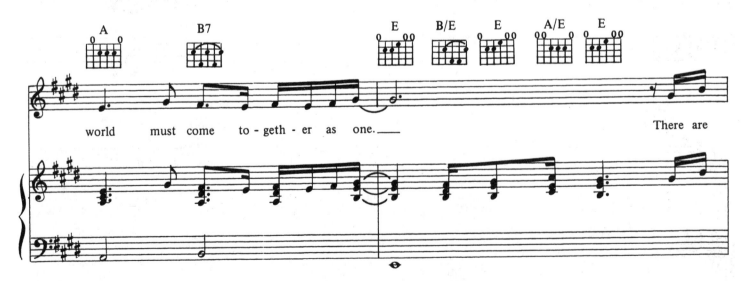

world must come to - geth - er as one. _____ There are

We Are the World - 6 - 1

WHEN I SEE YOU SMILE

Words and Music by
DIANE WARREN

Some-times I won-der if I'd ev-er make it through,— through this world_ with-out hav-ing you._

126

When I See You Smile - 9 - 3

128

When I see you smile, ___

1. ba - by, when I see you ___ smile at ___ me.

2. ba - by, when I see you smile ___ at me. Some-times ___ I wan-na

When I See You Smile - 9 - 5

130

THE WIND BENEATH MY WINGS

Words and Music by
LARRY HENLEY and JEFF SILBAR

The Wind Beneath My Wings - 7 - 1

136

138

YOU'RE THE INSPIRATION

Words and Music by
PETER CETERA and
DAVID FOSTER

love some-bod-y; till the end — of time; when you

love some-bod-y; al-ways on — my mind. no one needs — you more than I. When you

Repeat ad lib.
and fade

𝄉 *Verse 2:*
And I know (yes, I know)
That it's plain to see
We're so in love when we're together.
Now I know (now I know)
That I need you here with me
From tonight until the end of time.
You should know everywhere I go;
Always on my mind, you're in my heart, in my soul.

(To Chorus:)